Echoes of a Scorpio

Shawanna Denise

BookLeaf
Publishing

India | USA | UK

Presentation by *BookLeaf Publishing*

Web: www.bookleafpub.com

E-mail: info@bookleafpub.com

ISBN: 9789363307056

First edition 2024

*To those who persevere in the face of adversity,
heartbreak, and loss*

*who find strength in their vulnerability,
forgiveness, and healing*

*and who inspire others through their courage
and resilience.*

This book is for you.

ACKNOWLEDGEMENT

Thank you to everyone who believes in me and my divine purpose!

PREFACE

Welcome to "Echoes of a Scorpio," a collection of poetry and prose that delves into the depths of emotion and self-discovery. This book is born from the intense and transformative energy of a Scorpio, known for its profound connection to the hidden and mysterious facets of our inner worlds.

The Scorpio is a symbol of passion, resilience, and the power to transform. It guides us through the labyrinth of our deepest feelings, illuminating the shadows and revealing the truths we often keep hidden. This collection is a reflection of that journey—a journey of love, loss, healing, and rebirth.

As you turn these pages, you will encounter pieces that speak to the raw, unfiltered emotions that reside within us all. Each piece of writing is an invitation to explore the complexities of the human soul, to embrace vulnerability, and to find strength in the midst of transformation.

Writing this book has been a deeply personal experience, a way to navigate my own emotions and understand the world around me. I hope that in reading these words, you find echoes of your own experiences and emotions. May this collection offer you solace, inspiration, and a deeper connection to your own inner self.

Thank you for joining me on this journey. Let the Echoes of a Scorpio guide you to a place of introspection and growth, where you can embrace the power and beauty of your own inner world.

With love and light,

Shawanna Denise

Cassette Tape

I have you on my mind
Replaying those events
The words you would whisper to me when I
would vent.

And when you told me that you loved me
I kept replaying your voice over and over in my
head
The smoothness of your sound like thunder
mixed with rain.

I think about us all the time
Holding hands and chasing band$
We did everything together
It's crazy how things have changed.

And like a cassette tape, I keep rewinding.

I want to remember when you would hold me
when I was crying
The good ole' days when we didn't worry for
much
Oh, the good ole' days when all it took was a
touch
From you to make me feel better.

Over and over again,
I hear you loud and clear
Even in my dreams, you make yourself known
And like a cassette tape, I let you go on and on
And like a cassette tape, I keep rewinding.

Mason Jar

Tightly sealed but breakable
Void of all feelings.
For she has been hurt before
And felt the pain of not living.
Tucked away, shy, and avoidant
She doesn't want to be hurt again.
Betrayal is the worst.
It left her shattered, distant, and afraid.

Afraid to love again
Disappointed in what was and
Scared of what's to come.
Be brave young woman,
Be brave.
Unseal your heart
Let healing in.
To heal your wounds
To erase the pain.
Allowing your cracks to show
Displays vulnerability
Openness to move on
To let go of the past.

The past that no longer serves what is new to
come

Breakable we all are
Piece-able we can be
Put together so perfectly
Like we were created and free
Divine image
I see you as you glow.

All is not loss
You know the way to go.
From here it is up
Upward and onward
Let love show.
You are timeless
You are virtuous.
Molded-in an image that's
so crystal clear.
Preserved for the best;
unsealed yet breakable
She will love again.

I Will Not Be Your Sometimes

I will not be your sometimes
To call when she's upset.
I will not be your sometimes
The one you will regret.
I will not be your sometimes
To sleep with than forget.
I will not be your sometimes
To sneak away and text.
I will not be a sometimes
To another woman's man.
I will not be your sometimes
And cause another woman pain.
No, no I won't!
I will not be your sometimes.

How Long?

I often wonder how long I will have to go through this. How long will it take?

I find myself sitting in the bathroom crying my eyes out, feeling as if what I am doing is not enough and nothing is working.

Oh, why do my emotions take so much control over me?
Why aren't I brave enough? Nothing about me should be weak, but for him, I am.
How long must my soul mourn for a love that isn't the same?

I have to pull myself up from this pain.

My worth. I am valuable, no one can tell me differently. I am the change that I need to be, but again, I ask, how long?

I see myself coming out of this one day. One day soon. I know I don't have to be here. I have a plan. A plan to escape. To escape my thoughts and habits. I'll run as far away as I can, watch

and see, just watch and see, but, yet again, I ask,
how long?

Guessing

Guess where we are?
Not far

Your distant and cold heart is scared.

So, we stay
In the same place.

No growth
No worth
No escape

As dry as the dessert
Heart made of coal

I leave with my boundaries.
While you shield in your clove.

Forget You!

Forget you!

Forget you for leaving me
and Forget you for not believing in me.

Forget you and her
Forget you, fake and wannabes
This shit is personal.

Forget what we had
History means nothing.
Forget you and your indecisiveness.
You messy.
Forget you for playing with my heart
You petty.

Yeah, forget you!
I meant what I said
Yeah, forget you
for having her in your bed.

Forget your feelings and forget your heart
You made it hard for me to love again.
Forget you,
But I wish you well.

Emotions

Emotions need to flow.
I will not repress
I will let go and let the feelings flow.

Emotions can be cold.
Emotions can be bold
Emotions can be joyful
Emotions bring pain.

Emotions are feelings.
Emotions are love
Emotions are what we are
Emotions are how we navigate.

Emotions need to flow.
I will not repress
I will let go and let the feelings flow.

Emotions
Emotions
Emotions

What is this that I am experiencing?

Darkness

Into the dark, the deep and cornered walls are
where I choose to stay.
A place where I lay my head from the light that's
on display.
They are often the evil ones.
The ones who will betray.
The ones who smile in your face.
They're fake and full of hate.

Darkness is where I wish to lay
Away from the world
The pain, the suffering, and the loss.
I won't hide who I am.
I don't want your light.
I am fine.
Keep me hidden
I don't want to be found.

Please, show no remorse.
I chose this place
I've run my course.
Darkness is where I choose to stay
No one can find me here
It's better this way.

Please don't bring me your light
It's full of shame
Cause I know within you
There lies a flame
A flame that seeks to be hidden
Because it knows it's imperfect
A flame that wants to blow out
Because it's tired of searching.

Searching for truth,
That comes from within.
Which is why I remain in the darkness
I call it my friend.

All the Evil Man Cried

Run! Run! Run!
Into my circle of hope is what the evil man
cried. I'll give you all the knowledge and
understanding; there's nothing I will hide. Why,
indeed, you can trust in me. I'll provide you with
paradise. Just do as I say, think what I think, and
don't go astray. You can't do this without me;
you need my step each way. I'll teach you how
to pray, play, and even what to say.

Come! Come! Come!
Into my circle of hope is what the evil man
cried. You don't need anyone but me; you will
survive only with me. Chase after my sayings,
for it gives you life. Everlasting...what a price. I
know my teachings are fantasies and lies but you
need my structure in order to survive. Don't
stray. Just play in my little game of life. I
promise you rest, I promise you peace, I promise
you hope, come, come...you'll see.

3/11/19

I am lovable and deserve to be loved.

What a beautiful soul.

When my days seem weary, I look within. I am
resilient.
And when my nights feel lonely, it is I who give
liveliness.

I am learning to love myself and growing fonder
of me every day
And to let go of how others see and feel about
me, as I go my own way.

I am me, and I am enough!

Go Back

Don't come back
Do not turn around
Enter your paradise your island of love
Here, back home you lay awake desolate
Not happy, not secure, not at peace.

I wish I could give you what you need, but I
can't.
I can't love you the way you want me to love
you.
My heart has been open to change
My heart no longer lays open to chains- that
you've placed there when you left once before.

Don't come back here
I've shut down the harbor, your ships cannot
enter
Go back to your paradise
Where she treats you like an emperor.

Every Step of the Way

I am here for you every step of the way.
Hold my hand, and I will not leave you.

You are strong and beautiful.
Hold your head up high.

You are destined to be great.
Hold on to that feeling and watch how it
manifests.

You are uniquely designed to be special
I applaud you for your strength, dear one

Keep pushing and keep moving forward. There
is a lot in store for you
God has a plan for your life. You know it, you
feel it, be free. You're me

Distant

Out in space
I feel erased
Like I've been here before
This weird place.

I like it here
I don't have to wait on anyone
I don't have to talk to anyone or look up to
anyone.

It's nicer here
I shed no tear
I am accepted
I am not neglected.

I am love
I feel loved
I am connected
We are connected.

This inner peace is accepted.
I am one, we are one, interconnected.

Again

You are beautiful
Be great
Be you
Forget what others think
You are more than enough
I promise you that
Believe in yourself.
Great things will come
Again, I promise!

Beautiful Day

Today is beautiful as I sit by the ocean and soak up the sounds of the waves crashing to the surface. I hear God. I hear peace. My soul feels so good. I needed this.

Isn't it amazing how the sounds of nature sync well with your soul? I feel like I belong somewhere. My soul wishes to travel far. Wondering what's beyond the horizons of the sun, what's over the ocean's waves.

My soul yearns to be free. Freedom is what I seek. I am changing rapidly. My mind, my spirit, and my soul. I am blessed in many ways. I receive all that is meant for me. Through the darkness, I see the light; through the pain, I feel the love. The love that is one. A pure love. A love that I yearn to embrace FOREVER!

Gemini Man

Which twin will I meet today?
The one who is loving or the one who is cold?

Which twin will I meet today?
The one who wants to fuck or the one who
wants to cuddle?

Two is better than one.
So give me both
Just match my energy and do not go ghost.

Which twin will I meet today?
The one who texts good morning or the one who
leaves me on read?

Which twin will I meet today?
The one who smiles or the one who frowns?

Two is better than one, so I want both of you!

Toxic

Toxic, dare I like.
Mmmhmm, how he looks at me with those eyes
Starring deep into my soul, damn those eyes,
they get me every time
So fine and handsome
Oh, I like him
And those lips
His skin, his smile, smell, and dress
TOXIC…I know
But I like
I like his swag
He in his bag
I'm feeling him
Mmmhmm, he likes my ass
Boss bitch, yeah, he loves that
It'll be toxic; I know
He's feeling me though
But I like the thrill, the feels, and when we chill
Can I play in your hair?
Can I rub on your body?
So muscular.
Oh, I like your tattoos.
It's toxic. I know
Like poison running through my veins
Mmmhmm, he knows it too

Seductive, alluring, passionate, and clever
I love an intelligent man
But he'll be toxic, I know
How could I dare let go?
The warmth when we are together
He's serious and aloof
Fatal attraction
Damn, it will be toxic
I get it, I know

Forbidden Love

Forbidden love
I dare not touch
Forbidden love
Oh, it's a must.

The excitement of what's done in the dark
The excitement of forbidden love.

Forbidden love
Can I bite
A taste of your lips and a hint of your smell
I want to taste you

But….
You're a forbidden love.

No one has to know that you are my forbidden
and forever love
Hidden in secret, out of plain sight
You are mine despite you being my forbidden
love.

Fallen

I'm in love
I'm in love with you
You make me happy
You bring me joy
You make me smile

I have fallen
Fallen so deeply
What is this that I am feeling?
love, pure love that I want to give to you
Consume me, baby
Take over my soul

Existing

Existing until we exist
What does that mean?
No feelings
No strings
No emotions
We are just here
Existing until we exist.

A Short Story

Often, we don't know how much we've touched
someone's heart.
Whether it was just a casual fling, a hug, or a
ring-
By text or phone call is what I mean.
You begin to hold a special place in that person's
heart. It's unexplainable.
Like the universe sent them to you at the right
time and place.
Then, space occurred. Detachment too.
The feeling stays for a while because it was
deeper, you know.
Not the feeling of being deeply in love-
But the emotions of feeling safe.
Safe from the world and the pains of anxiety, as
if someone understood you without uttering a
word.
Short impressions leave lasting memories-
The memories that keep you up at night. The
memories that make you want to catch a flight.
No, not sex, though that was amazing
But HOME.
I will always have a friend somewhere between
the distance and the stars.

Don't do casual relationships, they say, and I
agree.
I don't want to fall-
Falling into feelings and emotions getting the
best of me.
He said he was here for a short time, not a long
time, and it was fun while it lasted.
But I see the bigger picture.
People come into our lives for many reasons; it
remains a mystery with you.
People run when they get scared but later feel
regretful-
That's me.
Persistent.
Feeling crazy, I know.
It's crazy to write this, but I hate to hold stuff in
So, I swallow my ego and pride.
No one likes rejection, but I get it.
On two different pages, one heart belongs to
another; busy, too
Some see it as it was...a fling. Others see it as it
was; spiritual.
He says there's nothing special about him- I beg
to differ.
A gentle and kind soul
Thank you for entering into my life
I wish you the best and much success

www.ingramcontent.com/pod-product-compliance
Lightning Source LLC
LaVergne TN
LVHW010838200726

843508LV00012B/2653